essential ell[a]

20 Ella Fitzgerald Classics

Production: Sadie Cook
Cover design by Watkiss Studios Limited

Published 1996

International Music Publications Limited
Griffin House, 161 Hammersmith Road, London W6 8BS, England

Due to copyright restrictions *Let's Face The Music And Dance* does not appear in this collection.

manhattan

Words by Lorenz Hart
Music by Richard Rodgers

with a song in my heart

Words by Lorenz Hart
Music by Richard Rodgers

ev'ry time we say goodbye

Words and Music by Cole Porter

11

the man I love

Music and Lyrics by
George Gershwin and Ira Gershwin

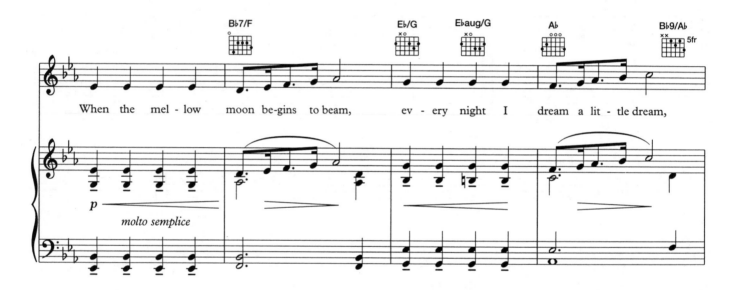

When the mel-low moon be-gins to beam, ev-ery night I dream a lit-tle dream,

and of course Prince Charm-ing is the theme, the he for me. Al -

a fine romance

Words by Dorothy Fields
Music by Jerome Kern

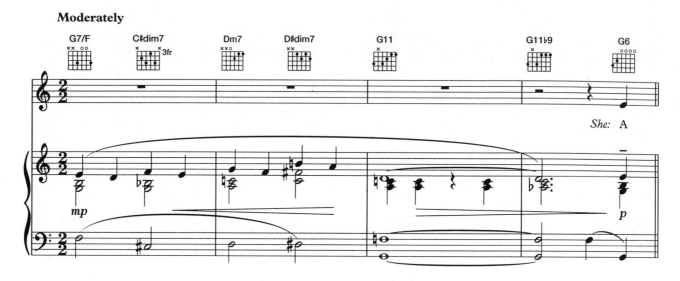

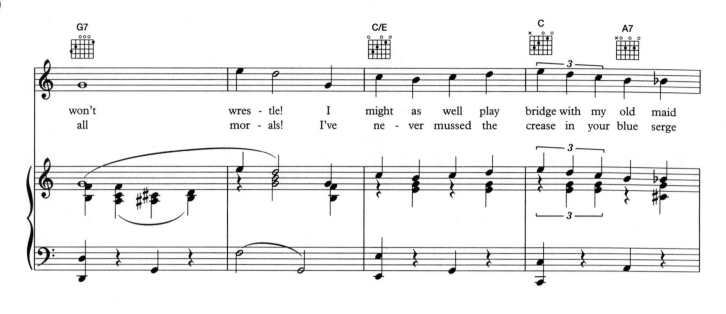

won't all wres - tle! I might as well play bridge with my old maid
mor - als! I've ne - ver mussed the crease in your blue serge

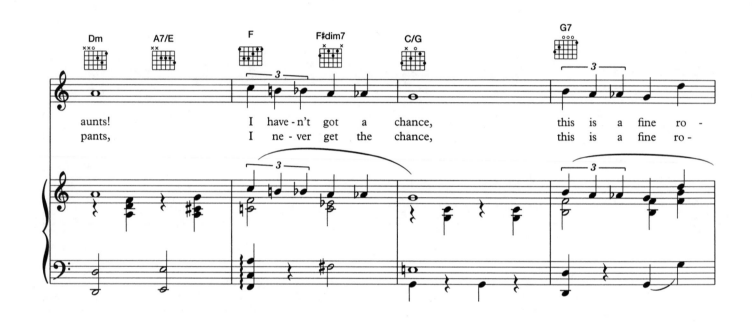

aunts! I have-n't got a chance, this is a fine ro -
pants, I ne - ver get the chance, this is a fine ro -

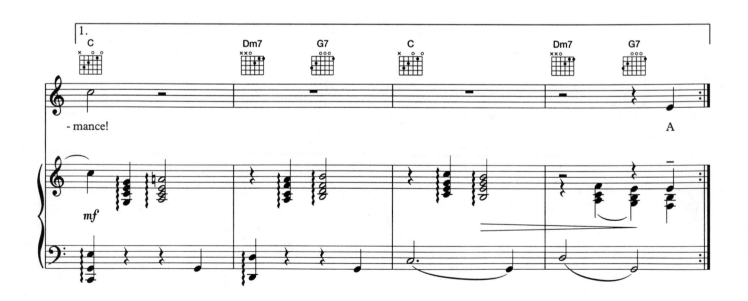

- mance!

A

blue moon

Words by Lorenz Hart
Music by Richard Rodgers

Once up-on a time, be -
Once up-on a time, my

mack the knife

Original Words and Music by
Kurt Weill and Bertold Brecht
English Words by Marc Blitzstein

let's do it (let's fall in love)

Words and Music by Cole Porter

I could write a book

Words by Lorenz Hart
Music by Richard Rodgers

love for sale

Words and Music by Cole Porter

it's all right with me

Words and Music by Cole Porter

what is this thing called love?

Words and Music by Cole Porter

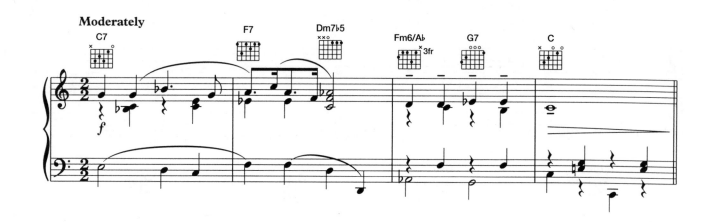

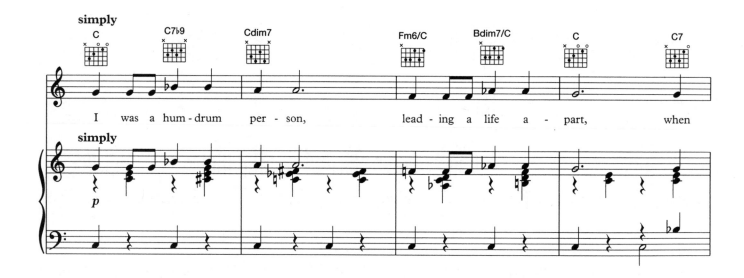

I was a hum-drum per-son, lead-ing a life a-part, when

love flew in through my win-dow wide, and quick-ened my hum-drum heart.

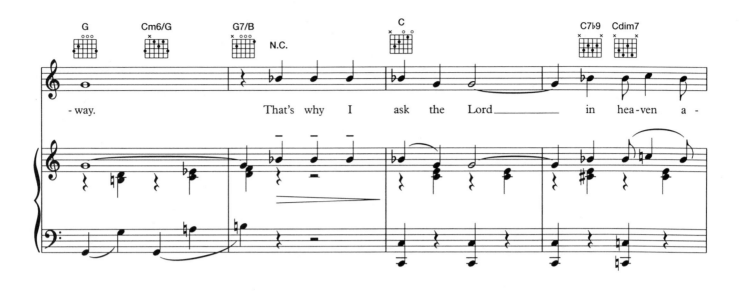

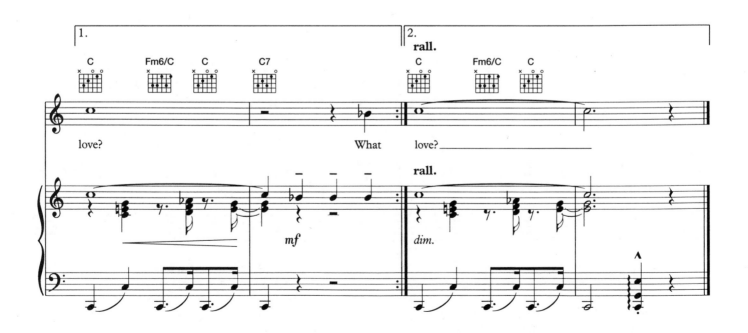

but not for me

Music and Lyrics by
George Gershwin and Ira Gershwin

REFRAIN Rather slow (*smoothly*)

's wonderful

Music and Lyrics by
George Gershwin and Ira Gershwin

VERSE

1. (HE) Life has just be - gun, Jack has found his Jill;
2. (SHE) Don't mind tell - ing you, In my hum - ble fash,

Don't know what you've done, But I'm all a - thrill.
That you thrill me through With a ten - der pash.

61

REFRAIN

let's fall in love

Words by Ted Koehler
Music by Harold Arlen
Additional Words by Charles Wilmott

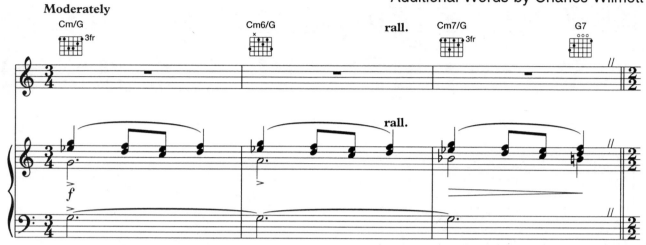

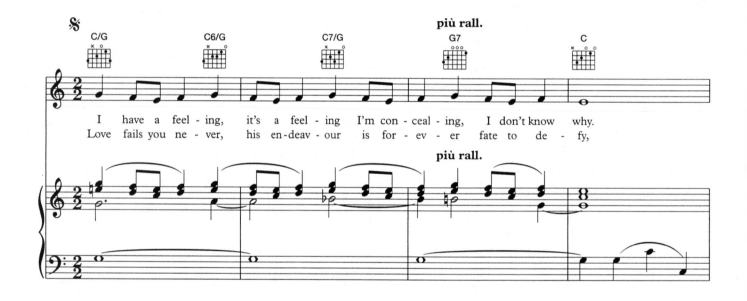

I have a feel - ing, it's a feel - ing I'm con - ceal - ing, I don't know why.
Love fails you ne - ver, his en - deav - our is for - ev - er fate to de - fy,

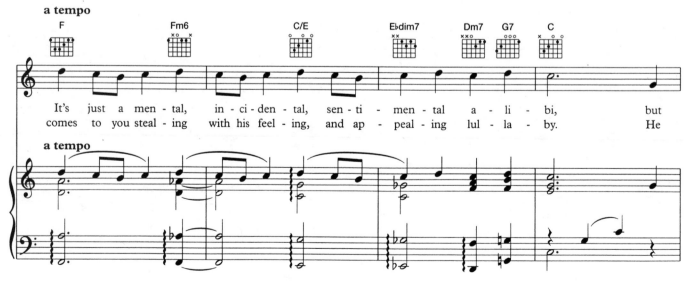

It's just a men - tal, in - ci - den - tal, sen - ti - men - tal a - li - bi, but
comes to you steal - ing with his feel - ing, and ap - peal - ing lul - la - by. He

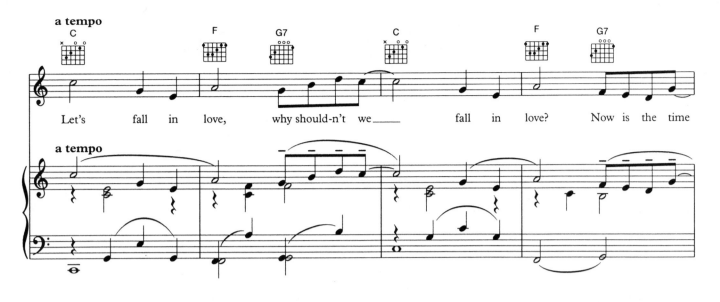

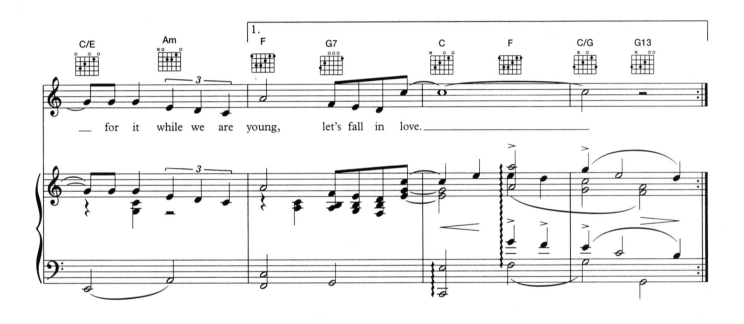

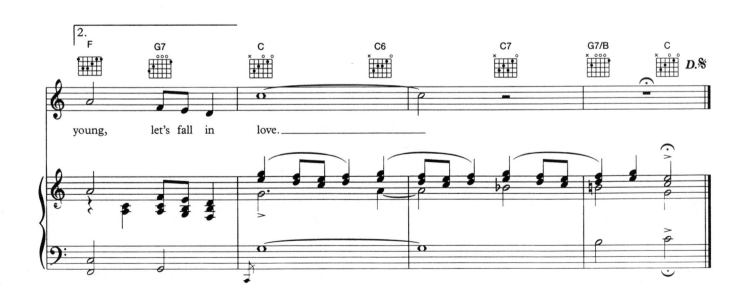

my funny valentine

Words by Lorenz Hart
Music by Richard Rodgers

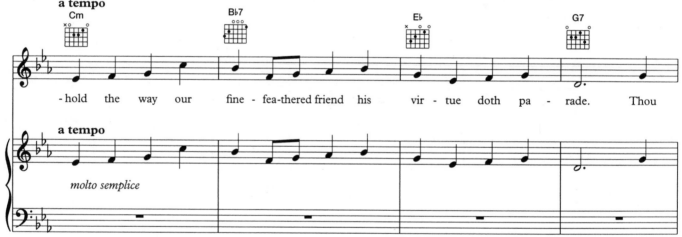

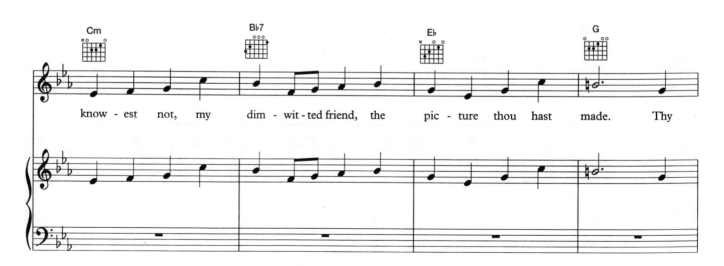

bewitched

Words by Lorenz Hart
Music by Richard Rodgers

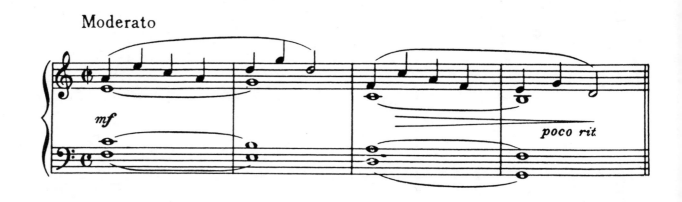

He's a fool and don't I know it, But a fool can have his charms;

I'm in love and don't I show it, Like a babe in arms.

there's a small hotel

Words by Lorenz Hart
Music by Richard Rodgers

I'd like to get a - way, Jun-ior, some-where a - lone with you.

It could be oh, so gay, Jun-ior! You need a laugh or two.

love is here to stay

Music and Lyrics by
George Gershwin and Ira Gershwin

82

the lady is a tramp

Words by Lorenz Hart
Music by Richard Rodgers

Printed by
Halstan & Co. Ltd., Amersham, Bucks., England